# Investing in Bitcoin Mining Stocks

*Andromeda Creations*

Copyright © 2024 Andromeda Creations
Todos los derechos reservados.
ISBN: 9798340806512

*"Bitcoin miners are the most important participants in the Bitcoin network because they're the guardians of Bitcoin's integrity and security."*

*Michael Saylor*

# CONTENT

| | | |
|---|---|---|
| | INTRODUCTION | 8 |
| 1 | THE BITCOIN ECOSYSTEM | 15 |
| 2 | WHAT ARE BITCOIN MINING COMPANIES? | 23 |
| 3 | KEY FACTORS TO EVALUATE BITCOIN MINING COMPANIES | 33 |
| 4 | RISK ANALYSIS IN INVESTING IN BITCOIN MINING COMPANIES | 43 |
| 5 | INVESTMENT STRATEGIES FOR BITCOIN MINING COMPANIES | 53 |
| 6 | LEADING PUBLICLY TRADED BITCOIN MINING COMPANIES | 63 |
| 7 | THE FUTURE OF BITCOIN MINING AND INVESTMENT OPPORTUNITIES | 81 |
| 8 | THE TRANSITION TO DATA CENTERS FOR ARTIFICIAL INTELLIGENCE (HPC) | 73 |
| | CONCLUSIONS: HOW TO CAPITALIZE ON THE GROWTH OF BITCOIN MINING | 86 |

# DISCLAIMER

The information contained in this document should not be interpreted as financial advice or as a recommendation to make investments.

This material is for informational and educational purposes only. The author will not be liable for any financial loss resulting from investment decisions made by the reader. All investments carry risks, and it is the responsibility of the investor to carefully assess any decision before committing capital.

Do your own research. Make sure to conduct your own independent analysis and do not rely solely on the information presented here or the opinion of third parties. All investment decisions should be made with full knowledge and at your own risk

# INTRODUCTION

The technological revolution of the 21st century has brought about numerous advances across all sectors of the global economy, but few have been as transformative as the rise of cryptocurrencies. Among them, Bitcoin has emerged as the undisputed leader, reshaping concepts of value, transaction, and trust within an interconnected global economy. Bitcoin is not only a decentralized digital currency but has also spawned an entire industry around it, with publicly traded Bitcoin mining companies playing a crucial role.

This introduction aims to provide an overview of Bitcoin, mining, and the investment opportunities presented by publicly traded mining companies. As we dive deeper into the upcoming chapters, we will explore how investors can engage with this emerging industry, what key factors are critical for success, and what challenges may arise. However, before delving into the technical details, it is essential to understand the fundamentals of Bitcoin and its relationship with mining.

**The Bitcoin Revolution**

In 2009, an anonymous developer or group of developers using the pseudonym Satoshi Nakamoto launched Bitcoin, the first cryptocurrency. What started as a technological experiment has grown into a global financial phenomenon that has changed the way people think about money. Bitcoin was designed as a decentralized electronic cash system that doesn't rely on central banks or intermediaries. Instead of trusting a central authority, Bitcoin uses blockchain technology, which enables direct, secure, and transparent transactions between users.

Since its inception, Bitcoin has been a highly volatile asset, experiencing dramatic spikes in value followed by sharp declines. Nevertheless, the overall trend has been one of sustained growth, with increasing adoption by both retail and institutional investors. This growth has fueled a rising demand for processing and validating transactions on the Bitcoin network, which has given rise to the mining industry.

**What is Bitcoin Mining?**

Bitcoin mining is the process by which transactions are validated and blocks are secured on the Bitcoin blockchain. Through a process called Proof of Work (PoW), miners solve complex mathematical problems that verify the legitimacy of transactions. In exchange for providing this validation service, miners are rewarded with new bitcoins, along with the fees associated with the transactions included in the block.

The concept may seem simple in theory, but in reality, Bitcoin mining is a resource-intensive process. As more miners join the network and competition to mine blocks increases, greater computational power is required to solve the mathematical problems necessary to validate transactions. This computational power is directly tied to the amount of energy a mining operation consumes, making electricity and specialized equipment (known as ASICs, or Application-Specific Integrated Circuits) critical factors in determining the profitability of a mining company..

## Publicly Traded Bitcoin Mining Companies

In Bitcoin's early years, mining was mainly done by individual enthusiasts using home computers. However, over time, mining has become more professionalized and is now dominated by large companies with industrial-scale facilities. These mining companies have set up operations with hundreds or even thousands of mining rigs, capable of generating vast amounts of computing power. Many of these companies have gone public, opening their operations to public investors.

Investing in these companies provides an indirect way to gain exposure to the Bitcoin market without having to buy the cryptocurrency directly. For investors who want to benefit from the rise of Bitcoin but may be concerned about the inherent risks of owning cryptocurrencies (such as secure storage and extreme volatility), mining companies offer an attractive alternative. Companies like Marathon Digital, Riot Blockchain, and Hut 8 have established themselves as key players in the industry, and by going public, they have allowed investors to participate in their growth. In the following sections, we will analyze some of the leading publicly traded mining companies.

## Why Invest in Publicly Traded Bitcoin Mining Companies?

The Bitcoin market is known for its volatility. Prices can rise or fall rapidly, which can unsettle traditional investors. However, Bitcoin mining companies offer a way to mitigate this volatility, as their revenue depends not only on the price of Bitcoin but also on factors like operational efficiency, electricity costs, and the technology they use.

Investing in a publicly traded Bitcoin mining company also provides transparency and regulatory oversight. Unlike many private companies or decentralized projects in the crypto space, publicly listed companies must adhere to strict regulatory standards, including the disclosure of financial and operational information. This allows investors to perform detailed analyses of the company's financial health and growth prospects.

On the other hand, it's important to recognize that these investments also carry risks. In addition to Bitcoin price volatility, mining companies face operational challenges related to high energy costs, the need for expensive and specialized hardware, and intense global competition. Mining companies are also exposed to regulatory changes, especially regarding energy consumption and environmental impact, which could affect their long-term profitability.

## Purpose of the Book

This book aims to provide a comprehensive guide for anyone interested in investing in publicly traded Bitcoin mining companies. Throughout the chapters, we will break down:

- What Bitcoin mining companies are, how they operate, and the challenges they face.
- How to evaluate mining companies in terms of financial, operational, and technological aspects.
- What factors influence the profitability of mining companies, from Bitcoin prices to energy costs and regulations.
- What investment strategies exist to capitalize on the growth of these companies.
- What best practices can help minimize risks and maximize opportunities in this emerging sector.

By the end of this book, readers will have a deep understanding of not only how publicly traded Bitcoin mining companies work but also how to make informed investment decisions in this sector.

The rise of cryptocurrencies, and specifically Bitcoin mining companies, has created a new world of opportunities for investors. However, it is also a complex and rapidly evolving space that requires a clear understanding of its dynamics and risks. This book will serve as a valuable tool for navigating this exciting, yet sometimes challenging, market.

Get ready to explore the fascinating world of Bitcoin mining companies and learn how to become an informed investor in this sector full of potential.

In the next chapter, we will explore in detail what Bitcoin is, how the underlying technology works, and why it has forever changed the way we understand global finance.

# 1 THE BITCOIN ECOSYSTEM

Bitcoin is much more than just a cryptocurrency; it is a disruptive technology that has captured the attention of governments, businesses, investors, and individuals worldwide. Its emergence has radically transformed how we understand money, transactions, and the global economy. To understand the role of publicly traded Bitcoin mining companies, it is essential to explore the broader ecosystem in which they operate.

In this chapter, we will discuss the history of Bitcoin, the technology behind it called blockchain, how mining works, and the challenges and opportunities that this ecosystem presents.

## 1.1. A Brief History of Bitcoin

Bitcoin was created in 2009 by an individual or group of people under the pseudonym Satoshi Nakamoto. In their whitepaper titled "Bitcoin: A Peer-to-Peer Electronic Cash System," Nakamoto proposed a decentralized digital currency that would allow direct transactions between users without the need for intermediaries such as banks or payment processors. This approach marked a fundamental shift from the traditional financial system.

Since its inception, Bitcoin has undergone significant evolution. Initially, only a small group of enthusiasts and programmers recognized its potential. However, as its adoption grew, so did its value, increasing from just a few cents in its early days to thousands of dollars today. This dramatic rise in value has attracted the attention of institutional investors, tech companies, and even governments, which have begun to consider it both as a store of value and as a new class of asset.

However, Bitcoin has not been without controversy. Its early association with illegal activities, such as the Silk Road black market, and its use in anonymous transactions raised concerns about regulation and its role in the economy. Despite these challenges, legitimate use of Bitcoin has grown exponentially, and it has been adopted by major corporations, payment platforms, and even nations like El Salvador, which has recognized it as legal tender.

## 1.2. Blockchain Technology

At the core of Bitcoin lies its underlying technology: the blockchain. This technology not only enables Bitcoin's existence but has also sparked a wave of innovation across various sectors. Understanding how blockchain works is key to grasping why Bitcoin is secure, transparent, and decentralized.

**What is Blockchain?**

Blockchain is a distributed ledger that publicly, securely, and decentrally records all transactions made on the Bitcoin network. Unlike traditional database systems, where a central authority (such as a bank) validates and stores transactions, in blockchain, transactions are verified by a network of independent participants known as nodes.

Each block in the chain contains a set of transactions and is cryptographically linked to the previous block, forming a chain of blocks that traces back to the genesis block (the first block ever mined). Due to the nature of the blockchain, any attempt to alter a previous block would immediately be detectable, as it would affect all subsequent blocks.

**Why is Decentralization Important?**

Decentralization is one of the most important features of Bitcoin and blockchain technology. Rather than relying on a single point of control, such as a central bank or financial institution, Bitcoin relies on the collaboration of thousands of nodes worldwide to maintain and verify the network.

This decentralized structure has several key benefits:

- Security: There is no single point of failure. To hack the network, an attacker would need to control at least 51% of the entire network's computational power, which is extremely expensive and practically unfeasible.
- Transparency: All transactions are public and can be verified by anyone. While the identities behind the transactions are pseudonymous, the transparency of the transactions builds trust in the system.
- Censorship resistance: Since there is no central

authority controlling the network, it is nearly impossible to arbitrarily censor or block transactions.

## 1.3. Bitcoin Mining

Bitcoin mining is the process by which new blocks are added to the Bitcoin blockchain and transactions are validated. To understand how this process works, it's essential to become familiar with the concept of Proof of Work (PoW).

**What is Proof of Work?**

Proof of Work is a consensus mechanism used by Bitcoin to ensure the security and integrity of the network. Miners, who are individuals or companies running specialized nodes, compete to solve complex mathematical problems that require significant computational power. The first miner to solve the problem earns the right to add a new block to the blockchain and receives a reward in Bitcoin for their efforts, along with the transaction fees included in that block.

This process is what's known as "mining," as miners are essentially "extracting" new Bitcoins. Currently, the reward for mining a block is 3.125 BTC (as of April 2024), although this number decreases every four years in an event known as Bitcoin halving, which we will discuss later.

## Mining Equipment: ASICs

In Bitcoin's early days, miners could use their personal computers or graphics cards (GPUs) to participate in mining. However, as competition increased, the mining process became more demanding, and specialized equipment known as ASICs (Application-Specific Integrated Circuits) was developed to mine Bitcoin more efficiently.

ASICs are much more powerful than conventional computers and can perform millions of calculations per second. However, they also consume large amounts of electricity, making the geographic location of mining operations crucial to a company's profitability. Those with access to cheaper energy sources (such as countries with abundant hydroelectric or wind resources) have a significant cost advantage.

## 1.4. Challenges and Opportunities in the Bitcoin Ecosystem

While the Bitcoin ecosystem is full of promise, it also presents a series of challenges for investors, mining companies, and the broader community. Below are some of the key challenges and opportunities.

### Challenges

- Price Volatility: Bitcoin has proven to be a highly

volatile asset, with price fluctuations that can change dramatically in short periods. This volatility can affect both investors and mining companies, as their revenues depend directly on the value of the Bitcoin they mine.
- Energy Consumption: Bitcoin mining requires a significant amount of energy, leading to criticism over its environmental impact. Many mining companies are responding to these concerns by utilizing renewable energy sources, but the debate over Bitcoin's sustainability continues.
- Regulation: As Bitcoin and other cryptocurrencies gain adoption, governments around the world are developing regulatory frameworks to control their use. Laws and regulations can vary significantly by jurisdiction, and mining companies must stay alert to regulatory changes that could impact their business.

## Opportunities

- Growing Institutional Adoption: As more institutional investors and large corporations adopt Bitcoin as a store of value or a means of payment, the demand for the cryptocurrency continues to rise. This directly benefits mining companies, as the demand for their "product" increases.
- Decentralized Finance (DeFi): The rise of decentralized finance platforms built on blockchain technology is increasing Bitcoin's relevance as a secure and reliable asset within

this expanding ecosystem.
- Technological Advances: As mining technology continues to evolve, with more efficient ASICs and more accessible renewable energy, mining companies will be able to reduce costs and improve profitability.

In conclusion, the Bitcoin ecosystem is complex, fascinating, and dynamic. Since its inception in 2009, Bitcoin has grown from an experimental project into one of the most exciting asset classes of the 21st century. Blockchain technology has proven to be a revolutionary solution for transparency and decentralization, while Bitcoin mining has evolved into a highly competitive and sophisticated industry.

This ecosystem presents both challenges and opportunities for investors and companies alike. In the following chapters, we will dive deeper into the role of publicly traded Bitcoin mining companies, how they operate, and what factors influence their success or failure.

# 2 WHAT ARE BITCOIN MINING COMPANIES?

As Bitcoin has grown and evolved, mining operations have shifted from being an individual activity carried out on home computers to becoming a large-scale industry dominated by Bitcoin mining companies that are listed on major stock exchanges worldwide. These companies not only play a crucial role in maintaining the Bitcoin network, but they also provide investors with a unique opportunity to gain exposure to the cryptocurrency market without having to purchase Bitcoin directly.

In this chapter, we will explore what Bitcoin mining companies are, how they operate, why they have chosen to go public, and what factors influence their profitability. By the end of this chapter, readers will have a comprehensive understanding of how these companies function within the Bitcoin ecosystem and what considerations investors should keep in mind when engaging with this sector.

## 2.1. Definition of a Bitcoin Mining Company

A Bitcoin mining company is a business dedicated to large-scale Bitcoin mining. Its primary activity involves using specialized equipment (mainly ASICs) to validate transactions on the Bitcoin network, add new blocks to the blockchain, and earn rewards in the form of Bitcoin for doing so.

Unlike individual miners, who may operate from their homes or small setups, large-scale Bitcoin mining companies typically have vast facilities housing hundreds or even thousands of mining devices. These facilities require not only advanced infrastructure but also access to vast amounts of energy, as Bitcoin mining is an extremely electricity-intensive process.

There are several approaches to large-scale mining:

- Private Mining: Companies that operate their own mining farms, managing both the infrastructure and the equipment.
- Cloud Mining: Some companies offer cloud mining services, allowing investors to rent computing power without having to purchase equipment or manage mining operations directly.
- Mining Pools: Groups of miners who combine their computing power to increase their chances of successfully mining blocks and then share the rewards earned.

## 2.2. Why Does a Bitcoin Mining Company Go Public?

In recent years, several Bitcoin mining companies have chosen to go public. This means their shares are traded on public stock exchanges, such as NASDAQ or the Toronto Stock Exchange, allowing investors from around the world to buy and sell stakes in these companies.

There are several reasons why a Bitcoin mining company might choose to go public:

## Access to Capital

One of the main benefits of going public is gaining access to larger amounts of capital. Bitcoin mining is a capital-intensive activity, requiring constant investment in new mining equipment, infrastructure maintenance, and high energy costs. By going public, companies can issue new shares to raise funds, enabling them to expand their operations and remain competitive in a rapidly evolving market.

## Increased Transparency and Trust

Going public also subjects the company to greater regulatory scrutiny and investor oversight. This requires companies to provide transparent financial information, which can increase investor confidence. Publicly traded Bitcoin mining companies must adhere to strict regulations, such as publishing quarterly and annual financial statements, undergoing external audits, and disclosing operational risks.

For investors, this means they can perform a more in-depth analysis of the company's financial health and make more informed decisions. This transparency is especially valuable in an industry like cryptocurrencies, where perceived risks are high, and information may be limited for private companies.

**Improved Liquidity**

For founders and early investors in a Bitcoin mining company, going public also enhances the liquidity of their holdings. Unlike a private company, where shares cannot be easily sold, in a public company, shares are traded daily on stock exchanges, allowing shareholders the opportunity to sell part or all of their investments at any time.

## 2.3. How Bitcoin Mining Companies Operate

Although all Bitcoin mining companies share the same goal of validating transactions and generating Bitcoins, their operations can vary significantly depending on their business model, the location of their facilities, and the technological strategies they employ. Below are the main factors influencing the operation of a Bitcoin mining company:

**Mining Equipment (ASICs)**

Mining hardware is one of the most crucial elements for the success of a Bitcoin mining company. ASICs (Application-Specific Integrated Circuits) are devices specifically designed to perform the mining function efficiently. The more powerful the hardware, the higher the chances a company has of solving the complex mathematical problems required to mine blocks.

Mining companies are in constant competition to acquire

and upgrade their ASICs to stay up to date with technological advancements. ASIC manufacturers, such as Bitmain and MicroBT, are the main suppliers of these devices, and the prices of ASICs can vary significantly depending on demand and the capabilities of the equipment.

**Energy Consumption and Location**

Electricity is the second-largest cost for Bitcoin mining companies, after mining equipment. Due to the large amount of energy required to operate ASICs, mining companies seek locations where electricity is cheap and abundant. Many mining operations are established in regions with access to renewable energy sources, such as hydroelectric or wind power, to reduce costs and minimize environmental impact.

Some of the most popular countries for mining operations include the United States, Canada, and Iceland, due to their access to inexpensive energy, favorable climates (which help cool the mining equipment), and stable regulatory frameworks.

**Block Rewards and Halvings**

Miners' rewards come from two main sources: block rewards and transaction fees. Every time a miner adds a new block to the blockchain, they receive a certain amount of Bitcoins as a reward. However, this amount decreases over time through a process known as halving.

Halving occurs approximately every four years and reduces the block reward by half. For example, in 2020, the block reward was 12.5 BTC, and after the halving that year, it was reduced to 6.25 BTC. In 2024, the reward has been reduced again to 3.125 BTC. This supply reduction mechanism is designed to control Bitcoin's inflation, but it also poses a challenge for mining companies, as they receive less Bitcoin for the same amount of work.

To compensate for the reduced reward, mining companies must improve their efficiency, reduce costs, or benefit from an increase in Bitcoin's price. Halving can have a significant impact on the profitability of mining companies, making long-term planning crucial.

**Diversified Revenue Streams**

While Bitcoin mining is the primary source of income for these companies, some publicly traded miners are beginning to diversify their revenue streams. For example, some companies are using their computing power to mine other cryptocurrencies, such as Ethereum or Litecoin, or are developing complementary services, such as renting out computing power to third parties.

Additionally, some Bitcoin mining companies are exploring the possibility of incorporating renewable energy solutions, selling excess energy to local power grids or utilizing unused energy in their operations.

## 2.4. Leading Publicly Traded Bitcoin Mining Companies

As Bitcoin mining companies gain prominence, several have established themselves as industry leaders. The top publicly traded mining companies include Marathon Digital Holdings, Riot Platforms, Hut 8 Mining, Bitfarms, CleanSpark, TeraWulf, Iris Energy, Cipher Mining, Bitdeer Technologies Group, Bit Digital, HIVE Digital Technologies, and Core Scientific.

We will delve into each of these companies in detail in Chapter 6.

**In conclusion**, publicly traded Bitcoin mining companies offer a unique opportunity for investors interested in gaining exposure to the cryptocurrency market without directly purchasing Bitcoin. These companies operate in a complex environment where factors such as electricity costs, hardware efficiency, regulation, and Bitcoin halving play crucial roles in their profitability.

By going public, these companies not only enhance their access to capital but also offer greater transparency and liquidity to investors. However, the inherent volatility of Bitcoin prices and the operational challenges involved mean that investing in these companies carries certain risks that must be carefully considered.

In the next chapter, we will explore the key factors investors should evaluate when assessing a publicly traded Bitcoin mining company, including its profitability metrics, management quality, access to cheap energy, and ability to adapt to a constantly evolving technological and regulatory environment.

# 3 KEY FACTORS TO EVALUATE BITCOIN MINING COMPANIES

Investing in Bitcoin mining companies can be a lucrative opportunity, but it also comes with a series of risks and challenges. For investors, it's essential to understand the factors that can influence the success or failure of these companies. In this chapter, we will explore the key factors that investors should assess before investing in a publicly traded Bitcoin mining company. We will examine aspects such as cost structure, management quality, technological infrastructure, expansion strategy, and the company's ability to adapt to changes in the regulatory environment.

## 3.1. Cost Structure: Energy and Equipment

One of the most crucial elements determining the profitability of a Bitcoin mining company is its cost structure, primarily made up of two key factors: energy consumption and mining hardware.

### Energy Consumption

Electricity is the largest operational expense for Bitcoin mining companies, and energy efficiency is essential to remain competitive. Mining requires vast amounts of energy as ASICs (Application-Specific Integrated Circuits) operate at full capacity to solve the complex cryptographic calculations needed to validate transactions.

Key factors to evaluate in energy consumption:

- Cost of electricity: Mining companies located in regions with low electricity rates, such as areas with abundant hydroelectric power or renewable energy sources, have a significant competitive advantage. Countries like Iceland, Canada, and parts of the United States (especially Texas) are known for offering low-cost electricity.
- Use of renewable energy: Companies that utilize renewable energy sources not only reduce costs but also address environmental concerns from investors. Transitioning to clean energy can enhance public perception and reduce energy price volatility.
- Energy efficiency: The efficiency of energy use, measured by the ratio between computing power and electricity consumption, is crucial. The latest generation ASICs are more energy-efficient, allowing companies to mine more Bitcoin per unit of energy used.

**Mining Hardware**

The hardware used by Bitcoin mining companies is another key factor impacting profitability. Competition among miners means that those with more advanced and efficient equipment have higher chances of success.

Key aspects of mining equipment:

- Computational capacity: Companies using high-capacity ASICs, such as those manufactured by Bitmain or MicroBT, have greater ability to process transactions and mine Bitcoin. Computing power is measured in terahashes per second (TH/s); the higher this figure, the more efficient the mining operation.

- Hardware lifespan: ASICs do not have an indefinite lifespan. As equipment ages, it becomes less efficient and less profitable. Therefore, it's important to evaluate how frequently a company updates its equipment and its hardware replacement strategy.
- Technological innovation: A company's ability to acquire state-of-the-art equipment before its competitors can be a crucial advantage. Companies with early access to technological innovations are often better positioned in the market.

## 3.2. Expansion Strategy and Scalability

For a publicly traded Bitcoin mining company to achieve long-term success, it must be capable of scaling its operations efficiently. As the cryptocurrency market grows and mining becomes more competitive, mining companies must find ways to increase their computing power without incurring excessive costs.

### Infrastructure Expansion

A mining company that can effectively expand its infrastructure will be able to increase its market share and capture a larger proportion of block rewards.

However, expanding infrastructure requires significant capital investments, so companies must strike a balance between growth and costs.

Key factors to consider:

- Ability to attract capital: Publicly traded mining companies that can raise capital through equity or debt offerings will be better positioned to expand their operations. Companies like Marathon Digital Holdings and Riot Platforms have used this approach to fund major expansions.
- Strategic location: The location of new facilities is crucial. Companies need access to cheap energy, favorable regulations, and an appropriate climate for cooling mining equipment. Cold areas or those with established energy infrastructure are ideal.

**Partnerships and Collaborations**

Another important strategy for expansion is collaboration with other companies in the ecosystem. Some Bitcoin miners have formed alliances with technology or energy companies to gain access to cutting-edge hardware or more competitive electricity rates.

## 3.3. Financial Health and Profitability

Evaluating the financial health of a Bitcoin mining company is essential for any investor. While Bitcoin mining companies may appear profitable during periods of high Bitcoin prices, their profitability can fluctuate significantly based on various factors.

**Revenue Analysis**

The primary revenue stream for a Bitcoin mining company comes from block rewards and transaction fees earned for validating blocks on the blockchain. However, revenue can vary depending on the price of Bitcoin and mining difficulty.

Key aspects to consider:

- Investments in energy and equipment: Companies with substantial investments in energy infrastructure and more efficient equipment tend to be better positioned to generate sustainable revenue.
- Diversification of income: Some mining companies are diversifying their revenue streams. For instance, some miners also offer cloud mining services, where third parties can rent computing power to mine cryptocurrencies.

**Operating Profit Margin**

The operating margin of a mining company is a key metric for measuring its profitability. Companies with high margins have controlled costs and are capable of generating profits, even when the price of Bitcoin drops. Operating margins are typically influenced by electricity costs, equipment maintenance, and infrastructure expenses.

**Cash Flow and Debt**

Positive cash flow indicates that a company has sufficient liquidity to fund its operations and expansion without needing to issue debt or shares. Companies with high levels of debt may face difficulties during periods when Bitcoin prices decline.

## 3.4. Management and Corporate Governance

A crucial aspect of the success of a Bitcoin mining company is the quality of its management. Mining companies need an experienced and competent leadership team capable of navigating both the technological industry and the volatile cryptocurrency market.

**Executive Team Experience**

It is important to assess the experience and track record of the executive team. A team with a proven history in cryptocurrency mining or related industries such as technology, finance, or energy is likely better equipped to anticipate and mitigate risks, as well as identify growth opportunities.

## Corporate Governance and Transparency

Publicly traded mining companies are subject to strict corporate governance standards. Investors should consider whether the company adheres to strong governance practices, such as publishing transparent financial reports, conducting regular audits, and managing shareholder interests responsibly.

## 3.5. Regulatory and Political Risks

The regulatory environment for cryptocurrencies is constantly evolving, and Bitcoin mining companies are no exception. As governments around the world consider how to regulate Bitcoin and other cryptocurrencies, mining companies must be aware of the risks and opportunities these changes may present.

### Changes in Regulation

Regulatory frameworks can vary significantly from one country to another. In some countries, Bitcoin mining is incentivized by low electricity costs and favorable regulations, while in others, it may be banned or heavily taxed. Unexpected regulatory changes can have a drastic impact on the operations and profitability of mining companies.

**Regulatory Compliance**

Publicly traded Bitcoin mining companies are subject to stricter regulatory requirements than their private counterparts. This may include compliance with environmental, tax, and data security laws. Companies that implement proactive regulatory compliance policies are better positioned to avoid penalties and mitigate long-term risks.

## 3.6. Bitcoin Price Volatility

The final factor, and perhaps the most important, is Bitcoin price volatility. While mining companies generate revenue directly through mining, their profitability is deeply affected by fluctuations in the price of Bitcoin. When Bitcoin prices rise, mining companies experience greater profits. However, a sudden drop in Bitcoin's price can significantly impact their margins.

**In conclusion**, investing in publicly traded Bitcoin mining companies can offer substantial opportunities, but it also requires thorough and careful analysis. Key factors that investors should evaluate include cost structure, expansion capabilities, financial health, management quality, regulatory environment, and cryptocurrency market volatility. Understanding how these factors affect a specific company will help investors make informed decisions and maximize their potential returns.

In the next chapter, we will delve deeper into the major

risks associated with investing in publicly traded Bitcoin mining companies, ranging from Bitcoin price volatility to regulatory and operational risks.

# 4 RISK ANALYSIS IN INVESTING IN BITCOIN MINING COMPANIES

Investing in publicly traded Bitcoin mining companies can offer attractive returns, especially during bullish cycles of Bitcoin price. However, this type of investment also carries significant risks that investors must carefully understand and evaluate before committing their capital. In this chapter, we will analyze the main risks associated with investing in publicly traded Bitcoin mining companies, including the inherent volatility of Bitcoin's price, as well as operational, regulatory, technological, and environmental risks.

## 4.1. Bitcoin Price Volatility

The most obvious and critical risk for Bitcoin mining companies is the volatility of Bitcoin's price. Since the primary revenue for miners comes from the Bitcoin rewards they receive for validating blocks on the blockchain, their profitability is directly linked to the market value of this cryptocurrency. Bitcoin's extreme volatility can lead to significant fluctuations in revenue and, consequently, in the profitability of these companies.

**Impact of Bitcoin Price Increases and Decreases**

- Price Increases: When Bitcoin's price rises, the rewards mining companies receive become more valuable. This scenario tends to attract more investor interest in the shares of these companies, potentially driving up their stock prices as well. Additionally, mining companies can sell the Bitcoins they mine in the market to

generate cash income, maximizing their profits.
- Price Decreases: Conversely, when Bitcoin's price falls, the BTC rewards lose value, reducing miners' profitability. In these scenarios, many mining companies face significant challenges, especially those with less efficient cost structures. The decline in Bitcoin's value can also negatively affect the stock prices of mining companies due to negative investor sentiment.

**Hedging and Mitigation Strategies**

Some publicly traded Bitcoin mining companies have started implementing hedging strategies to mitigate the risk posed by Bitcoin price volatility. This may include the use of financial derivatives such as futures or options, which allow companies to lock in a future selling price for the Bitcoin they generate. However, using these instruments can be costly and complex, introducing new risks into the company's financial management.

## 4.2. Operational Risks

Bitcoin mining companies face a variety of operational risks that can impact their ability to generate revenue efficiently and sustainably. These risks include hardware failures, disruptions in power supply, system cooling issues, and technological obsolescence.

**Hardware Failures in Mining Equipment**

Mining hardware, such as ASICs, is critical to mining operations. However, these machines are expensive, have a limited lifespan, and are prone to technical failures. If a mining company experiences significant hardware failures or a large-scale breakdown of its ASICs, its mining capacity can be drastically reduced, directly impacting revenue. Additionally, acquiring new hardware at scale can be both time-consuming and costly, further reducing operational efficiency.

**Power Supply Disruptions**

A stable power supply is essential for the continuous operation of mining farms. A disruption in electricity availability—whether due to grid failures or local energy issues—can completely halt mining operations, resulting in financial losses. Moreover, Bitcoin mining is highly energy-intensive, so any sudden increase in electricity costs can significantly affect the company's profit margins.

**Technological Obsolescence**

Bitcoin mining technology evolves rapidly, and mining companies must keep up with the latest hardware innovations to remain competitive. ASICs that are efficient today can become obsolete within months or years, forcing companies to make continuous investments in cutting-edge equipment. If a company fails to upgrade its technology in a timely manner, it risks falling behind its competitors, diminishing its ability to earn mining rewards.

## 4.3. Regulatory Risks

The regulatory environment for cryptocurrencies, including Bitcoin mining, is constantly evolving as governments worldwide seek to regulate the sector. Publicly traded Bitcoin mining companies must comply with regulations both in their home countries and in the regions where they operate their mining facilities. Unforeseen regulatory changes can pose significant risks for these companies.

**Government Regulation on Mining**

In some countries, Bitcoin mining has been banned or restricted due to concerns over energy consumption and environmental impact. For instance, China banned cryptocurrency mining in 2021, leading to a mass exodus of mining companies to other countries. Changes in energy policies, such as increased taxes or restrictions on energy use, can also negatively impact the profitability of mining companies operating in certain jurisdictions.

**Cryptocurrency Taxes**

Tax laws related to cryptocurrencies are also evolving. Some countries have implemented specific taxes on cryptocurrency mining or the sale of mined bitcoins. These taxes can reduce the net profitability of mining operations, forcing companies to adjust their sales strategies or seek locations with more favorable tax environments.

## Compliance for Publicly Traded Companies

Publicly traded Bitcoin mining companies must also comply with regulations applicable to publicly listed firms, including financial disclosure, audits, and adherence to financial security regulations. Any failure to meet regulatory requirements could result in penalties, loss of investor confidence, and a decline in stock value.

## 4.4. Environmental Risks

The increasing scrutiny on the environmental impact of Bitcoin mining is another significant risk that investors need to consider. Mining consumes large amounts of energy, and in some regions, this energy comes from non-renewable sources, increasing the carbon footprint of the industry. This has led to pressure from governments and environmental organizations for mining companies to adopt cleaner and more efficient energy sources.

## Reputational Impact

The use of non-renewable energy by Bitcoin mining companies can negatively affect their reputation, particularly in an investment environment where sustainability and corporate responsibility are becoming increasingly important to investors. Companies that fail to adapt to these demands risk losing support from institutional investors, who are increasingly focused on sustainable investment principles.

## Environmental Regulations

Environmental regulations around energy use may become stricter in the coming years. Some jurisdictions have already begun to regulate energy consumption for cryptocurrency mining or impose restrictions on carbon emissions. Mining companies that are not prepared to comply with these regulations may face fines, operational restrictions, or even facility shutdowns.

## 4.5. Geopolitical Risks

Bitcoin mining companies operating in multiple countries or regions are subject to geopolitical risks, particularly if their operations are located in countries with political or regulatory instability. Geopolitical conflicts, economic sanctions, or changes in trade agreements can affect a Bitcoin mining company's ability to operate efficiently.

### Political Instability

Political instability in countries where mining facilities are located can lead to unexpected regulatory changes, such as increased taxes, asset confiscation, or restrictions on importing mining equipment. Companies that rely on a stable political environment for their operations are more vulnerable to these risks.

## International Trade Restrictions

Since Bitcoin miners depend on the importation of hardware and technological components, any restrictions on international trade or economic sanctions imposed on countries where their suppliers operate can disrupt supply chains and increase operational costs.

## 4.6. Competition and Mining Difficulty

Another key risk is the growing competition within the Bitcoin mining industry. As more miners join the network, the mining difficulty increases, meaning that more computational power is required to solve the mathematical problems needed to validate blocks. This higher difficulty can reduce a mining company's chances of success, thereby decreasing its revenue.

### Technological Innovation by Competitors

Competitors that adopt more efficient and powerful technologies can capture a larger share of the market and reduce the portion of mining rewards available to less advanced companies. Companies that are unable to quickly and efficiently upgrade their technological infrastructure risk losing ground to their rivals, which can negatively impact their profitability.

**In conclusion**, investing in publicly traded Bitcoin mining companies offers significant opportunities but is not without considerable risks. Key factors such as Bitcoin price volatility, operational, regulatory, environmental, and geopolitical risks, as well as increasing competition in the industry, must be carefully evaluated by investors. A detailed approach to understanding these risks and the mitigation strategies implemented by mining companies can help investors make more informed decisions and balance risk with potential reward.

In the next chapter, we will discuss various investment strategies in publicly traded Bitcoin mining companies, including technical and fundamental analysis, the use of cryptocurrency mining ETFs, and how to diversify a portfolio with exposure to Bitcoin mining companies.

# 5 INVESTMENT STRATEGIES FOR BITCOIN MINING COMPANIES

Once investors understand the fundamentals of Bitcoin mining companies and the associated risks, the next step is to develop strategies to maximize returns and minimize risks. Given the inherent volatility of Bitcoin and the complexity of the mining sector, it is essential for investors to adopt well-planned approaches tailored to their risk profiles and financial goals.

In this chapter, we will explore various investment strategies in publicly traded Bitcoin mining companies, including technical and fundamental analysis, the use of cryptocurrency mining ETFs, portfolio diversification, and how to select between different companies in the sector. By the end of this chapter, investors will be better equipped to make strategic decisions in this volatile market.

## 5.1. Direct Investment in Publicly Traded Bitcoin Mining Companies

The most direct way to invest in Bitcoin mining companies is by purchasing shares of publicly traded companies. These stocks provide indirect exposure to Bitcoin since the revenues and profitability of mining companies are heavily dependent on the price of the cryptocurrency. However, buying individual stocks comes with specific risks, so conducting thorough research before making an investment decision is crucial.

## Fundamental Analysis

Fundamental analysis is a key approach to assessing the financial health of a Bitcoin mining company and its growth potential. This type of analysis involves reviewing the company's financial statements, balance sheet, cash flow, and long-term growth prospects. Some of the most important indicators to analyze include:

- Revenue and profit margins: Is the company generating sustainable revenue? How do its operating margins compare to those of its competitors?
- Debt levels: Companies with high levels of debt may be in a vulnerable position if the price of Bitcoin falls or operational costs increase.
- Expansion capacity: Does the company have a clear expansion plan to increase its mining capacity? Is it investing in new technologies and improving efficiency?
- Revenue diversification: Some mining companies are diversifying their income streams by mining other cryptocurrencies or offering blockchain-related services. Evaluating these additional sources of revenue can provide clearer insight into the company's long-term potential.

## Technical Analysis

Technical analysis involves studying price charts and historical patterns of stock prices to identify trends and possible entry and exit points. This approach is market behavior-based and can be useful for short-term investors looking to take advantage of volatility in Bitcoin mining stocks.

Key technical indicators to consider include:

- Moving averages: Simple or exponential moving averages (such as the 50-day or 200-day MA) can help investors identify long-term trends.
- Relative Strength Index (RSI): An indicator that measures whether a stock is overbought or oversold, potentially signaling price reversals.
- Trading volume: A spike in volume often indicates significant price movements. Investors can assess whether a trend has enough market participation to sustain its direction.

Combining technical analysis with fundamental analysis provides a comprehensive view, enabling investors to identify which Bitcoin mining companies offer the best investment opportunities and when is the best time to buy or sell.

## 5.2. Bitcoin Mining ETFs

For investors seeking exposure to the Bitcoin mining sector without concentrating their risk in a single company, exchange-traded funds (ETFs) can be an excellent option. These funds invest in a collection of shares from Bitcoin mining companies, allowing for risk diversification without the need to closely track individual companies.

## Benefits of Bitcoin Mining ETFs

- Diversification: An ETF provides exposure to several Bitcoin mining companies, which helps reduce the risk associated with company-specific issues.
- Access to a professionally managed portfolio: ETFs are typically managed by professionals who carefully select the companies included in the fund, offering an advantage in asset selection.
- Liquidity: ETFs are traded on stock exchanges just like individual stocks, providing high liquidity. Investors can easily buy and sell shares of the ETF during market hours.

## Risks of Bitcoin Mining ETFs

While ETFs offer diversification, they are not without risks. Since the stock prices of companies included in the ETF are correlated with the price of Bitcoin, investors remain exposed to the volatility of the cryptocurrency market. Additionally, management fees can reduce net gains over the long term, especially when compared to the direct purchase of individual stocks.

Some of the most popular ETFs offering exposure to the Bitcoin mining sector include:

- Global X Blockchain & Bitcoin Strategy ETF (BITS): An ETF that invests in companies related to blockchain and cryptocurrency mining.

- Valkyrie Bitcoin Miners ETF (WGMI): Focused specifically on companies engaged in Bitcoin mining.

## 5.3. Portfolio Diversification with Bitcoin Mining Companies

Given the volatility of cryptocurrencies and the highly competitive nature of Bitcoin mining, investors should consider diversifying their portfolios to mitigate risk. An effective way to do this is by combining investments in Bitcoin mining companies with other financial assets that are not directly correlated with Bitcoin or the cryptocurrency market.

### Investment in Technology-Related Sectors

Investors may consider adding technology companies that provide complementary services to the cryptocurrency sector. For example, companies like NVIDIA or AMD, which develop hardware for mining, can benefit from the growth of the mining sector without being exclusively dependent on Bitcoin's price.

### Investment in Commodities

Some investors opt to diversify with investments in commodities like gold, which are traditionally considered safe-haven assets. Since commodities like gold and Bitcoin often behave oppositely during periods of economic uncertainty, this can act as a hedging strategy against cryptocurrency volatility.

**Investment in Alternative Cryptocurrencies**

Another way to diversify is by investing in other cryptocurrencies such as Ethereum, BNB, or Solana. These cryptocurrencies may experience growth cycles independent of Bitcoin, offering a way to diversify within the cryptocurrency market itself.

## 5.4. Dollar Cost Averaging (DCA) Strategy

The Dollar Cost Averaging (DCA) method is an investment strategy where a fixed amount of money is invested in an asset (in this case, shares of Bitcoin mining companies or cryptocurrency ETFs) at regular intervals, regardless of the asset's price. This strategy helps reduce the risk associated with price fluctuations by averaging the cost of the shares over time.

**Advantages of DCA**

- Reduction of volatility impact: By investing a fixed amount of money consistently, investors avoid the temptation to "time" the market. This is especially useful in highly volatile markets like cryptocurrencies.
- Investment discipline: DCA encourages a disciplined approach, as investors continue to invest during both bull and bear markets. This can reduce the risk of panic selling during market

downturns.
- Lower average cost: During market downturns, DCA allows investors to purchase more shares at lower prices, potentially resulting in a lower average acquisition cost over time.

## 5.5. Market Timing and Bitcoin Cycles

One of the most challenging decisions for investors in Bitcoin mining companies is determining when to buy and when to sell. Given that Bitcoin's market cycles are notoriously unpredictable, attempting to "time" the market can be risky.

### Bitcoin Market Cycles

Bitcoin has shown a tendency to follow four-year market cycles, largely driven by its halving events. During these cycles, Bitcoin prices typically experience dramatic increases followed by significant corrections. Investors need to be aware of these cycles and adjust their investment strategies accordingly.

- Bull Cycle: Bitcoin prices rise rapidly, fueled by market enthusiasm and increasing institutional adoption.
- Bear Cycle: The market corrects after a bull cycle, leading to significant price declines. During these periods, Bitcoin mining companies with inefficient cost structures may face financial challenges.

## Exit Strategies

Deciding when to sell shares in a Bitcoin mining company can be just as important as determining when to buy. Some common exit strategies include:

- Staggered Selling: Investors gradually sell as share prices rise, allowing them to lock in profits while limiting risk.
- Profit Target Selling: Investors may set a specific profit target, such as selling when the stock price has risen by 50% or 100%.

**In conclusion**, investment strategies in Bitcoin mining companies should be based on a careful and diversified approach. From direct stock purchases to investing in mining ETFs or diversifying with related sectors, investors have various options for participating in this growing market. Understanding Bitcoin's market cycles, applying both fundamental and technical analysis, and adopting diversification strategies can help maximize investment opportunities while mitigating inherent risks.

In the next chapter, we will conduct a detailed analysis of the leading publicly traded Bitcoin mining companies, exploring their financial performance, operational strategies, and how they compare in the market.

# 6 LEADING PUBLICLY TRADED BITCOIN MINING COMPANIES

Now that we've explored the fundamentals of Bitcoin mining, its risks, and investment strategies, it's time to analyze some of the top companies in this sector. In this chapter, we will conduct a detailed case study of the leading publicly traded Bitcoin mining companies, examining their financial performance, operational strategies, and competitive advantages. This will give investors a clearer understanding of how these companies operate and what factors have helped them stand out in the competitive Bitcoin mining market.

## 6.1. Marathon Digital Holdings (NASDAQ: MARA)

### Overview
Marathon Digital Holdings is one of the largest and most well-known Bitcoin mining companies in the United States. Founded in 2010, the company initially focused on the patent industry but reinvented itself as a cryptocurrency miner in 2020, experiencing exponential growth since then.

### Mining Infrastructure and Capacity
Marathon operates large-scale mining facilities across multiple locations in the United States. By the end of 2023, the company had an operational hashrate exceeding 23 EH/s (exahashes per second), making it one of the largest miners globally. The company has secured competitive energy supply contracts in states like Texas, where electricity is cheaper and cryptocurrency mining is being actively promoted.

## Expansion Strategy

Marathon has pursued an aggressive expansion strategy, heavily investing in the acquisition of next-generation ASICs, allowing it to remain competitive in terms of energy efficiency. Additionally, the company has partnered with Compute North, a provider of mining and cloud storage solutions, to optimize operations and reduce operational costs.

## Financial Performance

Marathon's growth has been significant, driven by the rising price of Bitcoin and its ability to increase its hashrate. In 2023, its annual revenues surpassed $750 million, with relatively healthy profit margins. However, Marathon faces risks due to its high debt levels and heavy reliance on Bitcoin price volatility.

## Outlook and Challenges

Marathon remains one of the leading Bitcoin miners with a clear growth strategy. Nevertheless, it faces challenges related to technological competition, potential energy regulation in the United States, and Bitcoin's price volatility. The company has been investing in renewable energy to improve its long-term sustainability, which could help mitigate some of the regulatory and environmental risks.

# 6.2. Riot Platforms, Inc. (NASDAQ: RIOT)

## Overview

Riot Platforms is another leading Bitcoin mining company in the United States. Headquartered in Colorado, Riot has focused on building large-scale mining facilities in Texas, taking advantage of favorable energy costs and public policies. The company is also known for its commitment to sustainable mining, utilizing renewable energy sources.

## Mining Infrastructure and Capacity

Riot has significantly expanded its infrastructure. By the end of 2023, its operational capacity exceeded 13 EH/s. Its Whinstone facility in Texas is one of the largest cryptocurrency mining farms in North America. Additionally, Riot has secured long-term agreements for low-cost electricity, allowing the company to maintain a competitive edge in terms of operational costs.

## Expansion Strategy

Riot has pursued organic growth through the expansion of its facilities and the acquisition of new mining equipment. In 2023, the company invested over $500 million in purchasing next-generation ASICs, which has enhanced its operational efficiency. Moreover, Riot has implemented initiatives to use solar and wind energy, reinforcing its focus on sustainability.

## Financial Performance

In 2023, Riot generated over $600 million in revenue, positioning it as one of the most profitable Bitcoin miners in the market. However, like Marathon, Riot is highly dependent on Bitcoin's price, and its profit margins could be impacted by sudden market changes.

## Outlook and Challenges

Riot remains a leader in the Bitcoin mining industry in

terms of infrastructure and operational capacity. However, as it operates primarily in the United States, it is exposed to regulatory changes that could affect its profitability. Nevertheless, its focus on energy sustainability and continuous expansion positions it well to capitalize on future Bitcoin bull cycles.

## 6.3. Hut 8 Mining Corp. (NASDAQ: HUT)

**Overview**
Hut 8 Mining is a Bitcoin mining company based in Canada, known for its focus on sustainability and revenue diversification. Founded in 2017, Hut 8 has rapidly grown into one of the leading cryptocurrency miners in North America.

**Mining Infrastructure and Capacity**
By the end of 2023, Hut 8 operated with a mining capacity exceeding 8 EH/s. The company has facilities in Alberta and Ontario, where it benefits from inexpensive hydroelectric power, allowing it to operate with relatively low costs. Hut 8 has also invested in solar and wind energy, further improving its sustainability profile.

**Expansion and Diversification Strategy**
Hut 8 has been a pioneer in revenue diversification. In addition to Bitcoin mining, the company has ventured into the data center sector and cloud mining services. This diversification enables Hut 8 to generate income beyond the volatility of Bitcoin, providing a more stable financial profile compared to other miners that rely solely on cryptocurrency mining.

## Financial Performance

In 2023, Hut 8 reported revenues exceeding $200 million, a smaller figure compared to Marathon and Riot. However, its profit margins were stronger due to its focus on operational efficiency and income diversification. The company has been less dependent on Bitcoin's price thanks to its other revenue streams, allowing it to be more resilient during bear markets.

## Outlook and Challenges

Hut 8 remains one of the most sustainable and diversified Bitcoin mining companies in the market. Its ability to generate income beyond Bitcoin mining makes it less vulnerable to cryptocurrency market cycles. However, it faces challenges related to global competition and the need to keep up with the most efficient mining technologies.

# 6.4. Bitfarms Ltd. (NASDAQ: BITF)

## Overview

Bitfarms is a Bitcoin mining company based in Canada, known for operating multiple energy-efficient mining farms. The company strategically positions itself in areas with access to cheap and renewable electricity, enabling it to reduce its operational costs.

## Mining Infrastructure and Capacity

Bitfarms operates mining facilities in Canada, Paraguay, and Argentina, with a total mining capacity exceeding 6 EH/s by the end of 2023. The company has leveraged the low cost of hydroelectric power in these regions, giving it a significant cost advantage in terms of Bitcoin mined per dollar.

**Growth Strategy**
Bitfarms has followed a cautious expansion strategy, gradually increasing its operational capacity while keeping costs low. Unlike some of its competitors, Bitfarms has not aggressively invested in purchasing equipment, opting for a more sustainable growth model. Additionally, the company has expanded geographically to mitigate region-specific regulatory risks.

**Financial Performance**
In 2023, Bitfarms generated over $150 million in revenue, with an adjusted profit margin reflecting its focus on maintaining low operating costs. Although it is one of the smaller mining companies in terms of revenue, its energy efficiency and cost reduction strategy have positioned it favorably in the market.

**Outlook and Challenges**
Bitfarms has a solid outlook but faces challenges related to its growth capacity and the need to increase its hashrate to remain competitive in an expanding market. The company's strategy of geographic diversification aims to mitigate regulatory risks and enhance operational profitability.

## 6.5. CleanSpark, Inc. (NASDAQ: CLSK)

## Overview

CleanSpark is a Bitcoin mining company based in the United States, known for its distinctive sustainability-focused approach. Founded in 2014, CleanSpark combines Bitcoin mining with microgrid technology, enabling it to use renewable energy sources and optimize energy efficiency in its operations.

## Mining Infrastructure and Capacity

CleanSpark has experienced significant growth in recent years, reaching an operational hashrate of approximately 9 EH/s in 2023, with plans to increase this to over 16 EH/s by the end of 2024. Its operations are primarily located in the United States, especially in Georgia, where it takes advantage of access to cheap and renewable energy.

## Operational Strategy

CleanSpark has adopted an expansion strategy centered on sustainability. The company invests in microgrid technologies to optimize energy use, reduce operational costs, and minimize its carbon footprint. Additionally, CleanSpark has been investing in next-generation ASICs to improve energy efficiency and maximize production.

## Financial Performance

In 2023, CleanSpark generated approximately $220 million in revenue, with a focus on diversification through the implementation of advanced energy solutions. Its operating margins are strong, partly due to its commitment to energy efficiency.

## Outlook and Challenges

CleanSpark stands out for its focus on sustainability and energy innovation, which could attract institutional investors concerned with ESG (Environmental, Social, and Governance) criteria. However, like many mining companies, it remains vulnerable to Bitcoin price volatility, and its growth will depend on its ability to scale operations without significantly increasing costs.

## 6.6. TeraWulf Inc. (NASDAQ: WULF)

### Overview
TeraWulf is a Bitcoin mining company based in the United States, committed to operating with 100% carbon-free energy. Founded in 2021, TeraWulf has quickly gained traction due to its focus on sustainability and renewable energy-based operations.

### Mining Infrastructure and Capacity
TeraWulf operates facilities in New York and Pennsylvania, leveraging hydroelectric and nuclear energy. By the end of 2023, its operational hashrate had reached approximately 6 EH/s, with plans to continue expanding its capacity in the coming years.

### Operational Strategy
TeraWulf's strategy focuses on operating exclusively with clean energy, differentiating itself from other Bitcoin miners. By utilizing hydroelectric and nuclear power, TeraWulf keeps its operating costs low and avoids regulatory scrutiny often associated with the use of non-renewable energy.

**Financial Performance**
TeraWulf reported revenues of around $150 million in 2023, benefiting from its access to low-cost clean energy. While its profit margins are competitive, the company is still in a growth and expansion phase, which presents challenges related to financing its expansion plans.

**Outlook and Challenges**
TeraWulf offers an attractive proposition for investors seeking alignment with ESG (Environmental, Social, and Governance) criteria and viewing the growth of clean energy-powered Bitcoin mining as a long-term trend. However, as a relatively young company, it faces the challenge of solidifying its market position amidst growing competition.

## 6.7. Iris Energy Limited (NASDAQ: IREN)

**Overview**
Iris Energy, based in Australia, is a Bitcoin mining company that exclusively uses renewable energy for its operations. The company has been a strong advocate for sustainable mining, focusing on utilizing low-cost energy infrastructure in regions where renewable energy, such as hydroelectric power, is abundant.

**Mining Infrastructure and Capacity**
By the end of 2023, Iris Energy operated with a capacity of 5.6 EH/s in Australia and Canada, making it one of the leading Bitcoin miners that rely solely on renewable energy sources.

## Operational Strategy

Iris Energy's strategy focuses on leveraging geographic locations with access to hydroelectric and solar power, allowing the company to maintain low operational costs while meeting sustainability expectations. Iris Energy has made long-term infrastructure investments in Canada and other countries to capitalize on its clean energy-based operational model.

## Financial Performance

In 2023, Iris Energy generated approximately $180 million in revenue. Although smaller compared to some of the larger mining companies, its sustainability-focused approach has allowed it to attract institutional investors and maintain competitive margins.

## Outlook and Challenges

Iris Energy faces the challenge of scaling its operations efficiently while maintaining its commitment to clean energy. As investors increasingly value ESG (Environmental, Social, and Governance) criteria, Iris Energy stands to benefit from its sustainable focus. However, the company continues to face risks related to Bitcoin volatility and the need to expand its mining capacity.

## 6.8. Cipher Mining Inc. (NASDAQ: CIFR)

### Overview

Cipher Mining is a Bitcoin mining company based in the United States, focused on establishing highly efficient and scalable mining operations. The company was formed through a merger with Good Works Acquisition Corp. in 2021.

## Mining Infrastructure and Capacity
Cipher Mining operates with a capacity of approximately 6 EH/s and has been expanding its facilities in Texas, a region that has become a key hub for Bitcoin mining due to its low electricity costs and favorable regulatory environment.

## Operational Strategy
Cipher Mining's strategy revolves around leveraging long-term energy agreements in regions with cheap electricity, such as Texas. The company has secured contracts to obtain electricity at low costs, enabling it to maintain a lower cost per Bitcoin mined compared to many of its competitors.

## Financial Performance
Cipher Mining reported revenues of approximately $130 million in 2023. Its ability to secure low-cost electricity contracts and focus on operational efficiency has allowed the company to generate strong operating margins.

## Outlook and Challenges
Cipher Mining has a promising future if it can maintain its focus on operational efficiency and geographic expansion. However, its reliance on a favorable regulatory environment in Texas could pose a risk if energy policies change.

## 6.9. Bitdeer Technologies Group (NASDAQ: BTDR)

**Overview**
Bitdeer Technologies Group is one of the most innovative Bitcoin mining companies, with operations in multiple countries and a global presence. Founded by Jihan Wu, co-founder of Bitmain, Bitdeer specializes in large-scale mining and cloud mining solutions.

**Mining Infrastructure and Capacity**
Bitdeer operates with a global capacity exceeding 5 EH/s, with facilities located in North America and Asia. Its infrastructure is designed to be highly scalable, and the company also offers cloud mining services to both individual and corporate clients.

**Operational Strategy**
Bitdeer takes a dual approach: it engages in its own mining operations and provides cloud mining services. By allowing third parties to rent computing power, Bitdeer diversifies its revenue streams and reduces its reliance on Bitcoin prices, providing greater financial flexibility.

**Financial Performance**
In 2023, Bitdeer reported revenues exceeding $300 million, driven by both its direct mining operations and its cloud services. This diversified income stream gives Bitdeer a more stable profile in the face of Bitcoin price fluctuations.

**Outlook and Challenges**
Bitdeer is well-positioned for growth due to its access to

advanced technology and its global focus. However, competition in the cloud mining sector is increasing, and the company will need to continue innovating to stay ahead of the curve.

## 6.10. Bit Digital, Inc. (NASDAQ: BTBT)

**Overview**
Bit Digital is a rapidly growing Bitcoin mining company founded in 2015. Based in the United States, the company focuses on expanding its global operations, with facilities in North America and Asia.

**Mining Infrastructure and Capacity**
By the end of 2023, Bit Digital had an operational capacity of 3.6 EH/s and was working to expand its facilities in the United States and Canada. The company has secured agreements with energy providers to ensure reduced costs.

**Operational Strategy**
Bit Digital's strategy revolves around geographic expansion and optimizing operational efficiency through the acquisition of next-generation ASICs. The company has benefited from diversifying its geographic presence, operating in multiple countries to mitigate regulatory risks.

**Financial Performance**
In 2023, Bit Digital generated nearly $100 million in revenue. While it is one of the smaller mining companies compared to its competitors, its focus on expansion and

efficiency has allowed it to maintain reasonable profit margins.

**Outlook and Challenges**
Bit Digital has the potential for long-term growth, but it must continue investing in infrastructure modernization to remain competitive. Its ability to expand into new markets will be crucial for its future success.

## 6.11. HIVE Digital Technologies Ltd. (NASDAQ: HIVE)

**Overview**
HIVE Digital Technologies is a cryptocurrency mining company based in Canada that operates in the mining of Bitcoin and other cryptocurrencies. It was one of the first publicly traded miners to use renewable energy for its operations.

**Mining Infrastructure and Capacity**
HIVE operates facilities in Canada, Sweden, and Iceland, with a total hashrate of 3.4 EH/s as of the end of 2023. In addition to Bitcoin, HIVE has exposure to Ethereum, which diversifies its revenue streams.

**Operational Strategy**
HIVE's strategy is centered on cryptocurrency diversification and the use of renewable energy to maintain low costs and meet the expectations of institutional investors focused on sustainability.

**Financial Performance**

In 2023, HIVE reported revenues exceeding $160 million. Its ability to diversify its operations by mining multiple cryptocurrencies has helped stabilize its income during periods of Bitcoin volatility.

**Outlook and Challenges**
HIVE remains one of the most innovative and sustainable Bitcoin mining companies in the market. However, its focus on Ethereum also exposes the company to additional risks associated with the broader cryptocurrency market.

## 6.12. Core Scientific, Inc. (NASDAQ: CORZ)

**Overview**
Core Scientific was one of the leading Bitcoin mining companies in the United States and one of the largest globally before its recent financial restructuring. Founded in 2017, Core Scientific expanded rapidly, becoming one of the top Bitcoin mining companies by capacity. However, it faced financial difficulties, leading to bankruptcy in 2022. The company later restructured its debt and returned to growth.

**Mining Infrastructure and Capacity**
Before its restructuring process, Core Scientific operated with a hashrate exceeding 17 EH/s, positioning it as one of the largest mining companies in the world. Its operations were located in Georgia, Kentucky, North Carolina, and North Dakota, and the company had long-term energy supply contracts in place.

## Operational Strategy

Core Scientific adopted a strategy of accelerated growth, making massive investments in infrastructure and mining equipment. The company also offered hosting services to third parties, diversifying its revenue by providing facilities for other mining companies that did not want to own their own infrastructure. Core Scientific is currently transitioning its model toward High-Performance Computing (HPC), which we will analyze further in the next sections.

## Financial Performance

Core Scientific generated over $500 million in revenue in 2021. However, as Bitcoin prices fell in 2022 and operating costs rose, the company experienced liquidity issues that ultimately led to its restructuring. This process allowed the company to renegotiate its debts and continue operations while reconfiguring its financial structure. Recently, the company secured a multimillion-dollar contract in the HPC space, ensuring annual revenues of over €500 million for the next 12 years, enabling counter-cyclical investments in the Bitcoin sector (we will examine this case in more detail later).

## Outlook and Challenges

Despite its past financial struggles, Core Scientific remains a key player in the Bitcoin mining sector, boasting strong operational efficiency. The company is positioning itself as a leader in the market, pivoting toward artificial intelligence and HPC.

## 6.13. Conclusion

These companies represent a new wave of publicly traded Bitcoin miners adopting innovative approaches to compete in the sector. Some stand out for their focus on sustainability and renewable energy use, while others are diversifying their revenues through cloud mining services or mining multiple cryptocurrencies.

Each company offers unique advantages, from massive infrastructure and favorable energy agreements to diversified revenue streams and a focus on sustainability. However, they also face significant challenges related to cryptocurrency market volatility, regulatory changes, and technological competition.

For investors interested in this sector, it is crucial to evaluate not only the financial performance of these companies but also their ability to adapt to changes in the Bitcoin mining industry and their plans for the future.

In the next chapter, we will explore emerging trends and the future of Bitcoin mining. We will cover technological advancements, renewable energy adoption, and the opportunities that the development of new regulatory frameworks may bring.

# 7 THE FUTURE OF BITCOIN MINING AND INVESTMENT OPPORTUNITIES

Bitcoin mining has rapidly evolved from its early days, when enthusiasts used personal computers to mine blocks, into a global industry dependent on massive facilities and specialized equipment. As the Bitcoin market continues to grow and mature, the mining industry faces both challenges and opportunities that will shape its future.

In this chapter, we will explore emerging trends and the future of Bitcoin mining, focusing on technological advancements, the impact of renewable energy, regulatory changes, and other key dynamics that will influence investment opportunities in this sector.

We will save the discussion on the most important current trend—the transition of mining companies toward data centers for Artificial Intelligence (AI)—for the next chapter, as it is an intriguing topic that deserves its own section.

## 7.1. Technological Advances and Operational Efficiency

One of the most important factors shaping the future of Bitcoin mining is technological evolution. The development of more efficient and powerful mining equipment is crucial for companies to remain competitive and profitable in an environment where mining difficulty continues to rise.

## Next-Generation ASICs

ASICs (Application-Specific Integrated Circuits) are the most widely used devices in Bitcoin mining due to their ability to efficiently perform cryptographic calculations. As the market matures, major manufacturers like Bitmain and MicroBT continue to develop next-generation ASICs that promise to be faster and consume less energy.

- Increased energy efficiency: A key advancement will be the reduction in energy consumption. More efficient equipment can generate more computational power with less electricity, reducing operational costs for mining companies and increasing their profit margins.
- Higher computational power: New ASICs will also offer a higher hashrate (computing capacity) per unit, allowing mining companies to increase their capacity without needing to physically expand their facilities.

## Innovations in Cooling Systems

Cooling mining equipment is another critical aspect that affects operational efficiency. New liquid immersion cooling technologies allow miners to reduce the heat generated by ASICs and extend their lifespan. These solutions not only improve the performance of the equipment but can also reduce the energy costs associated with traditional cooling systems.

## Artificial Intelligence and Optimized Mining

The use of artificial intelligence (AI) to optimize mining operations is another emerging trend. AI-based solutions can monitor the performance of ASICs in real-time, detect issues before they occur, and adjust operational parameters to maximize efficiency. As AI becomes more integrated into mining operations, companies will be able to significantly reduce costs and increase profitability.

## 7.2. Impact of Renewable Energy on Bitcoin Mining

Energy consumption is one of the most controversial topics in Bitcoin mining. The increasing electricity demand to power mining operations has raised concerns about the environmental impact and carbon footprint of the industry. However, renewable energy sources are emerging as a key solution to address these challenges while enhancing the sustainability of mining operations.

### Hydroelectric, Solar, and Wind Energy

Many mining companies are relocating to regions where they can leverage renewable energy sources such as hydroelectric, solar, and wind power. Certain countries offer competitive access to these sources.

- Hydroelectric power: This is one of the most commonly used renewable sources by Bitcoin miners, particularly in regions with abundant water resources. Hydroelectric power is cheap, renewable, and stable, making it an ideal option for large-scale mining operations.

- Solar and wind energy: Although less consistent than hydroelectric power, solar and wind energy are gaining traction in Bitcoin mining. Companies operating in areas with abundant sunlight or wind are installing solar panels and wind turbines to reduce their reliance on traditional power grids and enhance their sustainability profiles.

**Government Incentives and ESG**

Governments are starting to offer tax incentives and subsidies to mining companies that use renewable energy or implement low-energy consumption technologies. These incentives could reduce operational costs and improve the profit margins of miners who adopt sustainable practices.

Additionally, mining companies that align with environmental, social, and governance (ESG) principles may attract more institutional investors seeking to meet their own sustainability criteria. This shift toward ESG-compliant operations could provide a competitive edge in a market increasingly focused on sustainability.

## 7.3. Regulatory Changes and Their Impact on Bitcoin Mining

The regulation of cryptocurrencies remains a topic of debate worldwide, and Bitcoin mining is no exception. As discussed earlier, governments are evaluating how to regulate the sector to address environmental, tax, and financial security concerns. Regulatory changes can have a significant impact on the mining industry, both positively and negatively.

**Tax Regulation**

Governments are developing tax frameworks for cryptocurrencies, including the imposition of taxes on mining activities. In some countries, Bitcoin mining may be subject to additional taxes on energy use or on the rewards earned from mining. Mining companies must be prepared to comply with these new tax requirements and adjust their financial strategies accordingly.

**Global Regulatory Framework**

On a global scale, the regulation of Bitcoin mining remains fragmented, but there is growing collaboration among governments to create more consistent standards. Some countries view Bitcoin mining as an economic opportunity, while others see it as a threat to their energy systems. The result will be a diverse regulatory environment where mining companies will need to operate flexibly and strategically.

Countries that promote Bitcoin mining through favorable energy prices and light regulatory burdens will likely become hubs for the industry. Conversely, countries that impose heavy restrictions or taxes may drive miners to relocate to more favorable jurisdictions. Miners must stay adaptable to navigate this evolving regulatory landscape while remaining compliant with local laws.

## 7.4. Opportunities in New Markets and Geographic Expansion

As Bitcoin mining continues to expand, new opportunities are emerging in non-traditional markets. Developing countries and regions with excess energy capacity are attracting mining companies looking to reduce costs and avoid competition in established markets.

### Emerging Markets

Countries in Latin America, Africa, and Central Asia are becoming hotspots for Bitcoin mining. These markets offer cheap electricity and, in some cases, governments that are willing to support the industry with tax or energy incentives. For example:

- Paraguay: Offers abundant and low-cost hydroelectric power, which has attracted several mining companies.
- Kazakhstan: Became a major mining hub after China banned Bitcoin mining. Its access to cheap energy and relatively favorable regulatory

framework make it appealing for mining operations.

**Geographic Expansion as a Risk Mitigation Strategy**

Geographic expansion is a key strategy for mining companies seeking to mitigate regulatory and operational risks. By diversifying their operations across different countries, companies can reduce their reliance on a single market or regulatory framework and safeguard against unforeseen changes in government policies. This approach not only spreads operational risks but also allows miners to take advantage of favorable conditions in multiple jurisdictions, whether in terms of energy costs, tax benefits, or regulatory leniency.

In addition to lowering risk, geographic diversification enables companies to scale more efficiently and tap into new opportunities as they emerge in various regions around the world.

## 7.5. The Bitcoin Halving and Its Effect on Mining

As we've discussed, the Bitcoin halving is one of the most significant events in the cryptocurrency ecosystem, and it has a direct impact on mining companies.

**Impact on Profitability**

Each halving reduces the amount of Bitcoin that miners can earn by cutting the block reward in half. This reduction puts pressure on mining companies to improve their efficiency or increase their hashrate to compensate for the lower rewards. While halvings have historically been followed by price increases in Bitcoin, mining companies must be prepared for a period of reduced profitability immediately after the event.

To navigate the challenges posed by a halving, miners often focus on optimizing their operations, reducing costs, and adopting more energy-efficient hardware. In cases where the price of Bitcoin doesn't rise as expected, less efficient miners may struggle to remain profitable, leading to industry consolidation where stronger companies absorb smaller, less competitive ones.

Long-term, however, miners who successfully adapt to the halving and optimize their operations could benefit significantly from potential price increases, making the halving a key event for strategic planning.

## 7.6. Investment Opportunities in the Future of Bitcoin Mining

As Bitcoin mining continues to evolve, new investment opportunities are emerging for those interested in the sector. Some key opportunities include:

**Investment in Renewable Energy**

The shift towards renewable energy in Bitcoin mining presents an attractive opportunity for investors interested in companies leading the charge towards sustainability. Companies that proactively adopt clean energy not only reduce their long-term operational costs but also appeal to institutional investors who prioritize Environmental, Social, and Governance (ESG) principles. This transition to renewables could help mining companies improve their profitability while meeting increasing regulatory and societal demands for sustainable practices.

**Investment in Technological Innovation**

Companies at the forefront of adopting cutting-edge technologies, such as next-generation ASICs and advanced cooling solutions, will likely emerge as long-term winners in the Bitcoin mining industry. Investing in companies that are leading in innovation and operational efficiency can offer significant returns as these technological advancements provide a competitive edge in reducing energy consumption and increasing computational power.

**Participation in Emerging Markets**

The rise of Bitcoin mining in emerging markets such as Latin America and Central Asia also offers promising opportunities for investors seeking geographic diversification. Companies that tap into these markets to reduce costs and avoid saturation in more mature regions will be well-positioned for long-term growth. Lower electricity prices and favorable regulatory environments in these emerging regions could boost profitability for mining companies operating there.

**In Conclusion**, The future of Bitcoin mining is full of both opportunities and challenges. Technological advancements, the increasing adoption of renewable energy, regulatory changes, and expansion into new markets are all factors that will transform the industry in the coming years. For investors, now may be the ideal time to get involved as the industry continues to grow and adapt to global trends.

Success in Bitcoin mining investment will require a deep understanding of operational and regulatory dynamics, as well as the ability to identify which companies are best positioned to navigate future changes and capitalize on growth opportunities.

# 8 THE TRANSITION TO DATA CENTERS FOR ARTIFICIAL INTELLIGENCE (HPC)

As the cryptocurrency market, and specifically Bitcoin mining, matures and faces challenges such as increasing mining difficulty, Bitcoin price volatility, and growing energy regulations, many leading publicly traded mining companies are seeking to diversify their operations. One of the most promising directions is the transition towards High-Performance Computing (HPC) data centers, focusing on providing infrastructure for the growing artificial intelligence (AI) market and other applications that require large amounts of data processing.

In this chapter, we will explore how and why publicly traded Bitcoin miners are evolving into HPC infrastructure providers, how artificial intelligence fits into this model, and what investment opportunities this emerging trend presents for investors interested in the sector.

## 8.1. Why Are Bitcoin Miners Transitioning to HPC Data Centers?

Bitcoin mining is a highly resource-intensive activity, particularly in terms of electricity consumption and computational processing. Mining farms require large amounts of computing power to solve the complex cryptographic problems that secure the Bitcoin network. However, these same computational capabilities can also be utilized for other technology applications that demand intensive processing, such as artificial intelligence, scientific simulations, and big data analysis.

Several reasons are driving publicly traded Bitcoin miners to diversify into the HPC and artificial intelligence market:

## Reducing Dependency on Bitcoin Prices

One of the biggest concerns for Bitcoin miners is their high dependency on the cryptocurrency's price. When Bitcoin's price falls, the profit margins of these companies are significantly impacted. By diversifying their revenue streams through providing HPC data center services for artificial intelligence, these companies can stabilize their income and mitigate the effects of cryptocurrency market volatility.

## Leveraging Existing Infrastructure

Bitcoin mining farms already have high-capacity infrastructure in place, such as advanced cooling systems, access to inexpensive energy, and redundant network connections. This infrastructure can be easily adapted to host servers that process AI tasks and other HPC applications. Companies can repurpose or expand their mining facilities to capture a new revenue stream without requiring significant capital investments.

## Exponential Growth in HPC Demand

The artificial intelligence and cloud computing markets are booming. Companies across all sectors, from technology to finance, need access to massive computational power to train AI models, run complex simulations, and process large datasets. Bitcoin miners are well-positioned to meet this demand by providing robust data centers that can handle these applications.

## Improving Sustainability Profiles

Bitcoin mining has been criticized for its high energy consumption. By diversifying into HPC and AI services, mining companies can improve their sustainability profile by optimizing energy use and reducing their reliance on the energy-intensive mining process. Additionally, by providing infrastructure for data analytics and AI, companies can more efficiently utilize renewable energy sources.

## 8.2. Artificial Intelligence and HPC: A Growing Market

Artificial intelligence, along with big data and machine learning, has become one of the fastest-growing technological fields over the past decade. These advancements require immense computational power, and AI applications can benefit from the idle capacity that Bitcoin miners can offer at their facilities.

### Artificial Intelligence Requires HPC

AI algorithms, particularly those related to deep learning, require advanced processors such as GPUs (graphics processing units) and other high-performance equipment. HPC data centers are essential for training large AI models and processing massive volumes of data. Bitcoin mining companies that already have high-performance infrastructure can adapt it to host these advanced servers, transforming into scalable data centers that support both cryptocurrency mining and AI applications.

**Sectors Demanding HPC**

In addition to AI, many other sectors are increasing their demand for HPC services, including:

- Finance: Financial market simulations and large-scale data analysis require significant computing power.
- Biotechnology and Healthcare: Medical research, drug development, and biological simulations use HPC platforms to perform complex calculations.
- Scientific Research: Fields such as astrophysics, climatology, and other sciences rely on high-performance computing to efficiently analyze data.

Bitcoin mining companies transitioning to HPC can capitalize on the demand from these sectors, further diversifying their revenue streams..

## 8.3. Bitcoin Mining Companies Leading the Transition to HPC

Several leading publicly traded Bitcoin mining companies have begun exploring the HPC data center market for artificial intelligence. Below, we analyze some of the companies at the forefront of this transition:

## HIVE Digital Technologies (HIVE)

HIVE was one of the first cryptocurrency miners to diversify into HPC and big data infrastructure. The company has begun offering its facilities to host HPC servers, focusing on applications such as financial modeling and artificial intelligence. HIVE's experience with cryptocurrency mining using renewable energy gives it a competitive advantage, as it can provide HPC services sustainably.

HIVE has indicated that it will continue expanding its capacity to serve companies seeking high-performance solutions, leveraging its existing infrastructure and expertise in data center management.

## Hut 8 Mining (HUT)

Hut 8 is another mining company that has taken significant steps toward diversification into HPC data centers. The company has established a specialized high-performance computing segment and has begun offering cloud services, including AI modeling and large-scale data processing.

Hut 8's ability to utilize its existing infrastructure and focus on energy efficiency has facilitated this transition. The company has reported growing interest from clients in sectors such as finance, biotechnology, and gaming, reflecting the broad range of applications that can benefit from HPC services.

**Core Scientific (CORZ)**

Core Scientific has started redirecting part of its capacity towards providing infrastructure for high-performance computing. The company has one of the largest data center infrastructures in the United States, with the ability to offer intensive processing services beyond Bitcoin mining.

Core Scientific has identified the artificial intelligence and big data market as a strategic opportunity to diversify its revenue streams and stabilize its financial position. By using its extensive facilities, Core Scientific is offering HPC services to companies requiring large-scale computing power.

At the end of this chapter, we will delve deeper into how this company is leading the transformation from Bitcoin mining to artificial intelligence, to understand how such a shift could affect the business and stock prices while serving as a model for other miners looking to adopt the same business strategy shift.

## 8.4. Challenges and Opportunities in the Transition to HPC

While the transition to HPC infrastructure offers numerous opportunities for Bitcoin mining companies, it also presents several challenges that need to be considered.

## Competition in the HPC Market

As more Bitcoin mining companies enter the HPC market, competition increases. Established cloud data center companies like Amazon Web Services (AWS) and Google Cloud already have a strong presence and global infrastructure to offer HPC services. Bitcoin miners will need to differentiate themselves, whether through lower costs, the use of renewable energy, or specialized services, to compete effectively in this space.

## Initial Investment and Adaptation

Although Bitcoin mining companies already have significant infrastructure that can be repurposed for HPC, a full transition still requires additional investments in equipment and technology. Adapting facilities to support the intensive processing demands of artificial intelligence may require upgrades in network connections, storage systems, and cooling technologies.

## Growing Demand

On the positive side, the demand for HPC and AI computing services is growing rapidly. According to market estimates, the demand for high-performance computing is expected to double in the next decade, driven by artificial intelligence, big data analysis, and the need for scientific simulations. Companies that can capitalize on this growing demand will be well-positioned to diversify and increase their revenue streams.

## 8.5. Investment Opportunities in Bitcoin Mining Companies Transitioning to HPC

The transition to HPC data centers presents an attractive opportunity for investors interested in the future of technology. Investors can benefit from several key areas:

**Diversification of Revenue Streams**

Bitcoin mining companies moving into HPC are diversifying their revenue sources, reducing their reliance on Bitcoin prices, and entering new, fast-growing markets such as artificial intelligence, data science, and academic research.

**Greater Financial Stability**

The HPC and AI services markets tend to be less volatile than the cryptocurrency market. Mining companies that successfully expand into these sectors can offer their investors greater income stability and predictability, potentially resulting in less volatility in stock prices.

**Capitalizing on Technological Trends**

Artificial intelligence and data processing are megatrends that are transforming the global economy. Companies positioning themselves as key infrastructure providers for these technologies can benefit from long-term growth in these sectors.

In summary, publicly traded Bitcoin mining companies

are making a significant transition toward becoming high-performance computing (HPC) data centers, capitalizing on the growing demand for data processing for AI and other intensive applications. This evolution offers an opportunity to diversify revenue streams, improve financial stability, and capitalize on the exponential growth of artificial intelligence and big data analytics.

While these companies will face competition from established cloud data center providers, their existing infrastructure and experience in large-scale operations provide them with a strategic advantage. For investors, this shift toward HPC represents a new growth avenue in the cryptocurrency sector, aligned with the most advanced technological trends of the 21st century.

## 8.6. Core Scientific's Contract with CoreWeave Encouraging Other Miners to Transition Toward Artificial Intelligence (AI)

Core Scientific (CORZ) has undergone a significant evolution in its business model in recent years, diversifying beyond Bitcoin mining. A key part of this strategy has been the signing of a contract with CoreWeave, a leading company in GPU infrastructure and cloud services for artificial intelligence (AI). This agreement is a central component in Core Scientific's transition toward becoming a provider of high-performance computing (HPC) data centers, focusing on AI and other computation-intensive applications.

Below, we explore how this contract with CoreWeave has

redefined Core Scientific's future, the growing importance of AI-related revenue, and how this shift has positively impacted its stock price.

### 8.6.1. The Agreement with CoreWeave: Strategic Diversification Toward AI

CoreWeave is a company specializing in offering GPU infrastructure and cloud services for AI, big data, and deep learning applications. Its focus is on meeting the growing demand for high-performance computing to train AI models, process massive data sets, and execute complex simulations. This demand is driven by the rapid adoption of AI across various industries.

The agreement between Core Scientific and CoreWeave aims to leverage the massive infrastructure that Core Scientific originally developed for Bitcoin mining. Thanks to its scalable data center infrastructure, Core Scientific can provide CoreWeave with the necessary computational capacity to support its cloud services, catering to businesses that require intensive data processing.

**Leveraging Existing Infrastructure**

The infrastructure already built by Core Scientific for Bitcoin mining, including its high-capacity energy facilities, advanced cooling systems, and network connectivity, is perfectly suited to meet the intensive computing needs demanded by AI applications. This means Core Scientific can diversify its revenue without needing to make significant investments in new infrastructure.

**Reducing Dependency on Bitcoin**

Traditionally, Core Scientific's revenue came almost exclusively from Bitcoin mining, a highly price-dependent activity. The volatility of the Bitcoin market has been one of the biggest risks for mining companies, unpredictably affecting their profit margins. The transition toward AI computing allows Core Scientific to reduce this dependency and offer services in a rapidly growing sector that is more stable and predictable.

### 8.6.2. Artificial Intelligence: The New Revenue Driver

Core Scientific has made it clear that it envisions a future where the majority of its revenue will come from services related to artificial intelligence (AI) and high-performance computing (HPC), rather than Bitcoin mining. This strategy is part of a broader movement within the cryptocurrency industry, where companies are seeking to diversify into more sustainable and less volatile sectors.

**Growing Demand for AI and HPC**

The artificial intelligence and high-performance computing market is rapidly expanding. Companies across a wide range of industries—such as biotechnology, finance, automotive, healthcare, and technology—are adopting AI models to enhance efficiency, decision-making, and innovation. All these advancements require massive amounts of computing capacity, which Core Scientific, through its partnership with CoreWeave, is well-positioned to provide.

- AI Model Training: Training deep learning models and other AI applications requires large volumes of data and processing power, which only massive data centers like those of Core Scientific can offer.
- Growth of Big Data: AI and big data analytics are driving increasing demand for HPC services, enabling the efficient processing and analysis of large datasets.

**Stability in Revenue**

Unlike Bitcoin mining, where revenue can fluctuate drastically depending on the price of the cryptocurrency, high-performance computing contracts and cloud services for AI tend to be long-term and more predictable. This allows Core Scientific to generate stable and recurring revenue, improving its financial profile and reducing the risks associated with cryptocurrency volatility.

**Positive Impact on Stock Price**

The signing of the CoreWeave contract and Core Scientific's transition toward AI-related revenue streams have had a positive impact on the company's stock price, which has risen from $3.5 to $10.

## Increased Investor Confidence

With this contract, investors now view Core Scientific not only as a cryptocurrency mining company but as a key player in the growing market for AI and HPC infrastructure. This perception has increased demand for the company's shares, driving the price up. Additionally, analysts have raised their growth expectations for the company, further adding upward pressure on its stock value.

## Future Outlook

Long-term expectations remain optimistic. With the AI market expanding and increasing demand for high-performance computing services, investors anticipate that Core Scientific could capture a significant portion of this market, enabling it to consolidate its position and generate substantial, more stable revenue compared to its previous reliance on the Bitcoin market.

## Investment Opportunities

Core Scientific's diversification into the AI and HPC market presents several opportunities for investors, particularly those looking for exposure to rapidly growing technology sectors with a focus on infrastructure.

## Exposure to Artificial Intelligence

AI is one of the most significant technological trends of the 21st century, and the demand for computing infrastructure for AI is booming. Investing in Core Scientific gives investors access to this growth, particularly in the cloud computing and high-capacity data center space.

**Risk Diversification**

By shifting its revenue focus toward AI computing and away from Bitcoin mining, Core Scientific offers investors a chance to reduce exposure to the volatility of the cryptocurrency market, providing a more stable and predictable income stream.

**Growth of the HPC Market**

The high-performance computing market is also growing rapidly, driven by applications in scientific research, financial analysis, AI simulations, and more. Core Scientific, through its existing infrastructure, is well-positioned to capitalize on this expanding market.

**In summary**, we may be witnessing the beginning of a widespread shift in the mining sector, with Core Scientific leading the way in this transition. In the final chapter, I will offer some closing thoughts on how investors can take advantage of the opportunities in this ever-evolving sector.

# CONCLUSIONS: HOW TO CAPITALIZE ON THE GROWTH OF BITCOIN MINING

Throughout this book, we have explored the fundamental dynamics that govern the Bitcoin mining industry, as well as the key strategies and considerations that investors should keep in mind. From analyzing the most prominent companies to assessing associated risks and growth opportunities, it is clear that Bitcoin mining is an expanding sector with the potential to generate significant returns, but also with considerable risks that require careful management.

In this final chapter, we will summarize the key points addressed throughout the book and offer a practical guide on how investors can capitalize on the growth of the Bitcoin mining sector while minimizing risks and maximizing their chances of success.

## 9.1. Future Opportunities in Bitcoin Mining

itcoin mining remains an evolving sector with numerous growth opportunities for both mining companies and investors.

### Technological Advancements

The future of Bitcoin mining will be shaped by technological innovations that enhance efficiency and reduce operating costs. Next-generation ASICs, advanced cooling solutions, and the use of artificial intelligence to optimize mining operations will be key factors that allow companies to remain competitive in an environment of increasing mining difficulty.

## Renewable Energy and Sustainability

The shift towards renewable energy will be a major driver for the sustainable growth of Bitcoin mining. Companies that invest in clean energy sources, such as hydroelectric, solar, and wind power, will not only reduce their long-term costs but will also be better positioned to meet future environmental regulations.
Additionally, initiatives aligned with environmental, social, and governance (ESG) principles will attract institutional investors looking for opportunities in sustainable sectors.

## Geographic Expansion

Mining companies that expand their operations into new markets with lower energy costs or favorable government incentives, such as certain countries in Latin America or Central Asia, will be able to access higher profit margins and mitigate regulatory risks in more mature markets.

## Opportunities in Integration with the Financial Sector

As cryptocurrencies continue to gain acceptance among institutional investors, Bitcoin mining companies could benefit from greater integration with the traditional financial sector. Collaborations with banks or investment platforms seeking exposure to the cryptocurrency market could open new revenue streams for mining companies.

## 9.2. How to Capitalize on the Growth of the Sector

Below are some key recommendations for investors to strategically and knowledgeably take advantage of the growth in the Bitcoin mining industry.

**Continuous Research and Evaluation**

The cryptocurrency market is dynamic and evolves rapidly. To maximize return potential, investors should conduct ongoing research on mining companies and external factors that may impact their performance. Staying informed about regulatory changes, technological advancements, and cryptocurrency market trends is essential.

**Portfolio Diversification**

Given the high risk associated with Bitcoin's volatility, it is advisable for investors to diversify their portfolios. A well-balanced strategy that includes both Bitcoin mining companies and less volatile assets (such as bonds or stocks from traditional sectors) can provide greater stability and protection against unexpected drops in cryptocurrency prices.

**Monitor Market Cycles**

Bitcoin halvings and market cycles are key events that can affect mining profitability. Investors should be aware of these cycles and adjust their buying and selling strategies accordingly. Purchasing during periods of low prices, such as in a bear market, and selling during bull cycles can help maximize profits.

**Leveraging Volatility with Long-Term Investments**

While Bitcoin mining is a volatile industry, investors with a long-term outlook may reap significant benefits by holding steady through periods of market instability. Mining companies that can withstand market downturns and adapt to technological and regulatory changes will be well-positioned to thrive in the future.

## 9.3. Final Thoughts

Investing in publicly traded Bitcoin mining companies presents a unique opportunity in the dynamic and ever-evolving world of cryptocurrencies. As Bitcoin continues to solidify its position as an important asset class, cryptocurrency mining companies have emerged as key vehicles for those looking to gain exposure to the sector without directly purchasing the cryptocurrency.

Throughout this book, we have explored the fundamental and strategic aspects investors must consider when evaluating Bitcoin miners. From analyzing hashrate and energy efficiency to understanding technological trends like the adoption of renewable energy and the use of artificial intelligence (AI), we have broken down the factors driving these companies' success.

One of the most exciting aspects of this sector is its

constant evolution. What may seem like a challenge today—such as high energy costs or cryptocurrency market volatility—can become tomorrow's opportunity. Bitcoin miners have begun diversifying their revenue streams and optimizing their operations, adopting cutting-edge technologies that not only improve profitability but also prepare them for the future.

This book has highlighted multiple opportunities for investors looking to expand their portfolios in the cryptocurrency space through solid, publicly traded companies. However, it is equally important to consider the inherent risks in this industry, such as Bitcoin price fluctuations, emerging regulations, and disruptive technological advancements like quantum computing.

In summary, investing in publicly traded Bitcoin mining companies is not just a bet on Bitcoin but also on the future of blockchain technology, renewable energy, and high-performance applications. With an informed strategy and a deep understanding of market trends, this sector offers one of the most exciting long-term opportunities for investors.

The future is uncertain, but it is also full of possibilities for those who can identify and capitalize on these opportunities. The time to explore the world of Bitcoin mining and its potential is now!

www.ingramcontent.com/pod-product-compliance
Lightning Source LLC
Chambersburg PA
CBHW050315230526
45471CB00005B/2190